ABSOLUTE BEGIN

CW00558511

Percussion

Wise Publications
part of The Music Sales Group
London/New York/Paris/Sydney/Copenhagen/Berlin/Madrid/Hong Kong/Tokyo

Published by
Wise Publications
14-15 Berners Street, London W1T 3LJ, UK

Exclusive Distributors:
Music Sales Limited
Distribution Centre, Newmarket Road, Bury St Edmunds,
Suffolk IP33 3YB, UK

Music Sales Corporation
257 Park Avenue South, New York, NY 10010, USA

Music Sales Pty Limited
20 Resolution Drive, Caringbah, NSW 2229, Australia

Order No. AM994015
ISBN 978-1-84772-588-2

This book © Copyright 2010 Wise Publications,
a division of Music Sales Limited.

Written by Hilko Shomerus
Music processed by Hilko Shomerus
Cover and book design by Tilo Müller
Printed in the EU

Your Guarantee of Quality:
As publishers, we strive to produce every book to the highest commercial standards.
The music has been freshly engraved and the book has been carefully designed to
minimize awkward page turns and to make playing from it a real pleasure.
Throughout, the printing and binding have been planned to ensure a sturdy,
attractive publication which should provide years of enjoyment. If your copy fails
to meet our high standards, please inform us and we will gladly replace it.

www.musicsales.com

Contents

Introduction

Welcome to the world of percussion! This book and audio/visual package will introduce you to the basics of Latin American rhythm, Afro-Cuban music and their native instruments.

This beginner's guide covers basic explanations of posture and rudimentary playing techniques while introducing the important rhythms of Afro-Cuban music.

The single most important rhythmic concept in Latin American music is the *clave* (a music instrument and rhythmic pattern that is used to organize the rhythms of the other instruments). Therefore, the specially-designed, play-along CD includes the music examples as audio demos with additional video presentations for a better learning experience.

While many musicians, and fans alike, consider the congas the most important percussion instrument in this style of music, it is important to understand the claves and the role that the clave pattern plays in Afro-Cuban music before exploring the other instruments. For this reason, this book features the congas as an equal part of the entire percussion family.

You will also be introduced to the most significant Cuban instruments and their use in the cha-cha-chá and mambo. In addition, playing in the 6/8 time signature is also discussed.

There is also a section that discusses the prevalent influence that Afro-Cuban music has on jazz, pop, rock, and folk. You will also find useful tips for performing in other musical styles or simply when gathering around a campfire.

This easy-to-follow method shows you:

- The most significant instruments in Afro-Cuban and Latin American music
- How to hold and play your instruments properly
- How to play different accompaniment patterns
- Tips and tricks for each instrument
- And lots of audio and video tracks for each instrument on the enhanced CD

! Try to practise a little every day, rather than a lot once a week. Practise as much as you can with the play-alongs or one of your own CDs. For better results, practise slowly!

Let's begin with explanations of common symbols and signs. Standard notation is used as much as possible to make explanations easy to understand; however, when writing for congas, for example, only two lines are used. This requires different symbols above or below the lines that indicate playing techniques and directions of movement respectively. With a little practice you'll be able to easily understand the rhythms and follow the symbols.

Congas:
OT = Open Tone
CS = Closed Slap
F = Finger
LP = Low Palm

Timbales:
◯ = Segundo ringing
● = Segundo muted
CB = Cha-Cha Bell
MB = Mambo Bell
Rim = Paila

Bongos:
TFT = Thumb & Fingertip (thumb resting, fingertip playing)
FT = Fingertip
F = Finger
OT = Open Tone
T = Thumb

Maracas:
> = Attack accent (hit on top and underneath)

!An **A** indicates an audio file, and a **V** indicates a video file on the play-along CD.

Güiro:
↓ = Quickly downward
↑ = Quickly upward
↓ = Slowly downward
↑ = Slowly upward
↓↑ = Quickly down, slowly up

Campana:
M = Striking the mouth
F = Striking the foot

Shaker:
→ = Forward motion
← = Backward motion

Tambourine:
→ = Moving to the right
← = Moving to the left
LP = Low Palm
FT = Fingertip

General Symbols:
r = Right Hand
l = Left Hand
> = Accent (tambourine, maracas or shaker)

Instrumentation

The Clave

Claves are a musical instrument of Cuban origin and are classified as a member of the percussion family. They consist of two manufactured, cigar-shaped pieces of hardwood. Like many African instruments that appear in pairs, the two claves are each given a gender: the *macho* (or male) is about 8 inches long while the *hembra* (or female) is half an inch shorter. They produce a short, dry sound that does not ring or resonate and can be surprisingly loud when played correctly.

The hembra is held in the left hand, which is slightly cupped underneath to form a resonant air pocket. It is then hit with the macho (held in the right hand) to create a sharp "click" that will cut through practically any ensemble. The goal is to keep everyone rhythmically together.

> ❗ *Claves* (plural) refers to the instrument while *clave* (singular) means the rhythmic pattern.

Wooden Claves

The rhythm pattern that the claves create is referred to as the clave pattern or, quite simply, *la clave*. This rhythm pattern is not an expressive part, but rather a lop-sided metronome that provides a rhythmic spine that keeps the rhythm patterns of the other instruments organized.

The word *clave*, in Spanish, means several different things: It can refer to the clef sign, keyboard, key, password, or code. However, when speaking of *la clave* in Cuban music, it specifically means the rhythmic part that is played by the sticks in popular music. This clave pattern does not need to be played to still exist and be understood.

Fibreglass Claves

Rhythm Patterns for the Claves

Although there are many different clave patterns, the most significant one is the *Son* clave. The Son clave is based on the *cinquillo*, or five-note, rhythm pattern that first came into prominence in the 1850s dance orchestras in Havana. These rhythms had emigrated to the city from the eastern parts of the island, most notably, Santiago de Cuba.

The pattern itself is a two-bar sequence that suggests three beats in the first bar followed by two beats in the second bar—also known as the 3:2 clave. It is also common to invert the pattern and have two beats in the first bar followed by three beats in the second bar, creating the 2:3 clave.

> ! Try to find words or syllables that fit with the rhythms and say them out loud while playing. This is a good way of learning and understanding these rhythm patterns.

The Son or 3:2 Clave

A 1: 3:2 Son Clave
V 1: 3:2 Son Clave

(Pa - na - ma   Pa - na - ma   Pa - na - ma   Ku - ba)

The Son or 2:3 Clave

If you turn around the 3:2 clave, the result is the 2:3 clave.

The 6/8 3:2 Clave

A2: 6/8 Clave
V2: 6/8 Clave

The following is the most common variation of the 6/8 or 12/8 clave. It can also be inverted and played as a 2:3 pattern.

Instrumentation

The Congas

The congas originated in Africa where, in many cultures, the drums had a deeply religious meaning and were only played on special occasions. These barrel-shaped hand drums were made out of wood, and the modern-day conga grew out of this tradition. The drums were introduced into Cuban culture from the Afro-Haitian culture, where they were played sitting down and were known as the *tumbadores de rumba*. These differed from the congas that were carried with a shoulder strap during parades and dance parties. Eventually, the new construction led to the *tumbadora* (or conga drum).

Today's three-drum ensemble that represents the popular conga set consists of the following:

The *tumbadora*, at 12 1/2 inches in diameter, has the deepest pitch of the three.

The *salidor* or *seis por ocho* is 11 3/4 inches in diameter and is the mid-pitched drum.

The *quinto* (short for *requinto*), at 11 inches in diameter, produces the highest pitch.

! The conga drum is emblematic of Cuban music; however, in 1929 Mayor Desiderio Arnaz banned congas from being played in public. Ironically, Dr. Desiderio Arnaz is father of the famous conga-playing singer and bandleader Desi Arnaz, Jr.

Sitting position

Sitting position (Quinto inclined)

The "Closed Slap" (CS), e. g. in improvisation

The "Closed Slap" (CS) with helping hand, e. g. in the "Tumbao"

The "Fingertip" (F); may also be played with palm resting

The "Low Palm" (LP)

Instrumentation

"Open Tone" (OT), played on the quinto

"Open Tone" (OT), played on the tumbao

Rhythm Patterns for the Congas
The Tumbao in 4/4

The *tumbao* is an *ostinato* (or repeating pattern) that is played on the conga set (usually the *tumbadora* and *salidor*) while rhythmic improvisations are performed on the *quinto*. It also happens to be the most important and most popular rhythm for the congas. It is vital that the tumbao lock with the clave pattern.

The Cuban Technique

A 3: Congas Cuban Tumbao
V 3: Congas Cuban Tumbao

This technique is the most widely used in Cuba, as well as the most commonly applied technique in Latin America. It is often called the "floating-hand" technique from the see-saw movement created by the left hand. The pattern combines the "low palm" (LP) and "finger" (F) which results in the left hand playing two to three strokes in a row.

The New York Technique

V 4: Congas Modern Tumbao

The author learned the following tumbao from the Puerto Rican percussion master, Freddie Santiago. This pattern originated in New York and definitely sounds more salsa and less Son.

The Tumbao in 3/4 or 6/8

A 4: Congas 6/8 Tumbao
V 5: Congas 6/8 Tumbao

The following example of the author's variation on the tumbao in 3/4, 6/8 or 12/8. This same hand pattern can also be found in a rhythm called *Bembè* (named after an orchestral work that incorporated religious aspects of African music mixed with Latin American folklore).

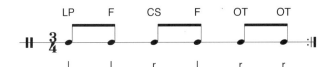 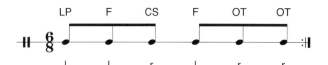

The Swing Technique

A 5: Congas Swing Tumbao
V 6: Congas Swing Tumbao

This technique can be used for playing swing, jazz or reggae. The hand patterns and playing techniques remain the same except for the triplet feel. Listen to the audio track and you'll immediately feel the grouping of three.

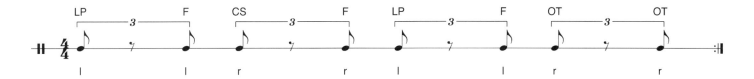

! Similar interpretations are also possible for many other conga hand patterns.

Instrumentation

The Congas in Cha-Cha-Chá

A 6: Congas Cha-Cha-Chá
V 7: Congas Cha-Cha-Chá

This one-bar hand pattern should, musically speaking, be felt over two bars. The tempo is rather slow, however, the cha-cha-chá bell pattern creates a strong, marching character.

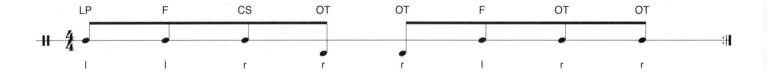

LP   F   CS   OT   OT   F   OT   OT

l   l   r   r   r   l   r   r

> ! The previous rhythms can easily be played on two drums. Notice that the open tones sound equally as impressive on the lower drum.

The Congas in Mambo (Cuban Hand Pattern)

A 7: Congas Mambo
V 8: Congas Mambo

Like the tumbao (or cha-cha-chá rhythm), this conga pattern is one of the most popular around the world. This two-bar phrase has a double-time feel and is widely used in a variety of styles. Also notice that the tempo is somewhat faster and more flowing than the cha-cha-chá.

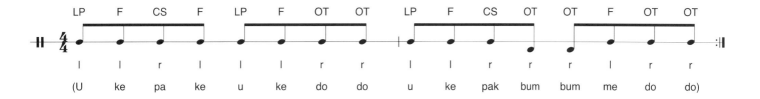

The Congas in Mambo (New York Pattern)

This tumbao pays homage to Freddie Santiago and is a modern interpretation of the mambo. The first bar contains a phrase from an already well-known tumbao. The second bar imitates the cha-cha-chá hand pattern from earlier on. This two-bar combination is often used when playing a mambo. The sound and technique are only slightly different from the Cuban version.

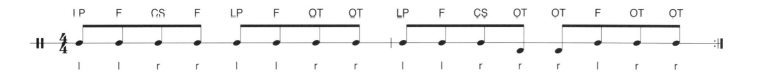

CHECKPOINT

What you have learned so far...
You have now learned the importance of the clave rhythm. You can perform basic techniques on one, two and three congas. Plus, you understand traditional and modern hand patterns for the congas that can be used in a variety of playing styles and time signatures.

Instrumentation

The Bongó

The *bongó* was an innovative instrument that entered Cuban popular music. Although it had its roots in Africa, the bongó originated in Cuba and added a touch of modern flair to Cuban folklore. Despite its easily portable size, the bongó was capable of loud, penetrating sounds with a versatility that was suitable for laying down complex rhythms.

The smaller drum is called *macho* (male) and the larger one is called *hembra* (female). The player is called a *bongosero*, and will often alternate with other small percussion instruments such as the campana during a piece of music.

The bongó are held steadily between the left inside knee (macho) and the right lower leg (hembra). They are played mainly using the fingers, however, it is not uncommon to witness players using sticks.

> ! The bongosero is capable of playing two-tone rhythms on the two heads while improvising like the *congero* on the quinto.

Sitting position (right-handed)

The "Thumb-Fingertip" (TFT)

The "Finger" (F)

The "Fingertip" (FT)

The "Thumb" (T)

The "Open Tone" (OT) on the hembra

In American pop culture, the bongó became known as the "bongo drums" or simply "the bongos." This was somewhat of a modern joke as it became part of the repertoire of beatnik clichés.

Instrumentation

Rhythm Patterns for the Bongó
The Martillo

A 8: Bongó Martillo Cha-Cha-Chá (70 bpm)
A 9: Bongó Martillo Mambo (100 bpm)
V 9: Bongó Cha-Cha-Chá
V 10: Bongó Mambo

The *martillo* (or "hammer") is the most popular hand pattern used in Cuban music and, as such, has been adopted by a variety of music styles that benefit from this light and relaxing rhythm. Keep in mind that slower to medium tempos (cha-cha-chá) are accented on every crotchet, while at a faster tempo (mambo) the "FT" (played on the second beat) loses its accent, creating the galloping feel that is so typical of the martillo.

C H E C K P O I N T

What you have learned so far...
You have learned the basic beats and rhythm patterns for the bongó—the *martillo*; in addition, a basic pattern for the 6/8 rhythm. You should now try the play-along exercises on the CD and experiment with your own variations. Don't worry about mistakes, just try to stay in time with the rhythm.

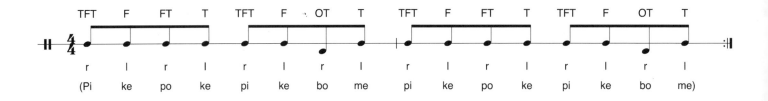

Basic Rhythm for the Bongó in 6/8 or 12/8

A 10: Bongó 6/8
V 11: Bongó 6/8

This 6/8 bongó rhythm can also be found in the book *Latin-American Percussion* by Birger Sylsbrück. It creates a relatively simple pattern for rhythmic accompaniment that is reminiscent of a blues-style bass line.

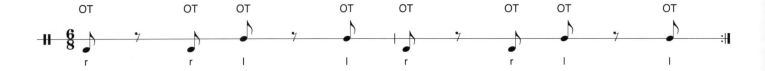

The Timbales

The *timbales* (or *paila*, which translates to "frying pan") are a pair of single-headed metal drums dating back to the early 1800s Cuban dance orchestras. The original set was made of wood which gave way to the copper (or steel) open-bottom cylindrical shape of today. The drums are fastened to a stand that also holds several cowbells (cha-cha-chá and mambo bell), as well as a wood or jam block. Also, you will often find a crash or ride cymbal.

Like African instruments, they are a sexed pair of slightly different sizes. The smaller and higher pitched drum is called *primero* or *macho*. It is located on the right-hand side, as opposed to the drum kit. The larger and lower drum is called *segundo*, or *hembra*, and is located on the left-hand side.

The *timbalero* plays this instrument standing up, hitting the drums (and also the rims) with special sticks. The timbales have been an important part of Cuban music since the late 1800s when they were a member of the *orquesta típica* (typical orchestra) that played the *danzón* (a style that grew out of the contradanza and the danza that became the Cuban national dance).

> ! The timbales adapted with the changing times and, in the 1920s, were an integral part of the *charanga* bands. Later, they continued to evolve and became a prominent member of the New York Salsa scene in the 1950s and '60s.

Instrumentation

The timbales stand with cymbal, playing position in the chorus (córo)

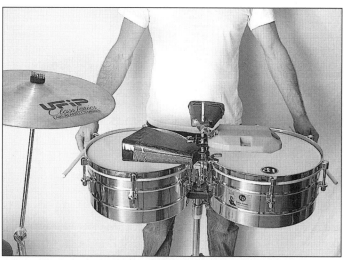

The timbales stand, playing position in the verse (pregón)

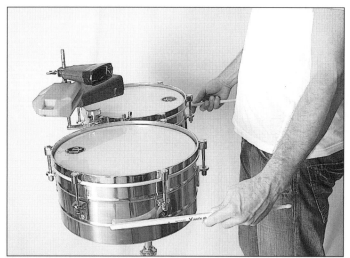

The standard "paila" (P)

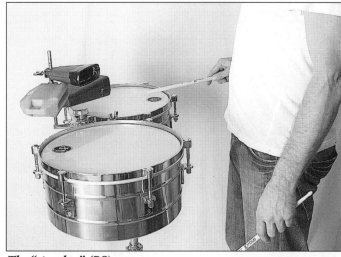

The "rim shot" (RS)

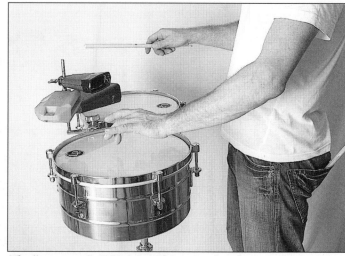

The "open tone" (OT) (segundo), using hand

The "closed tone" (CT) segundo, using hand

The "open tone" (OT) segundo, using stick

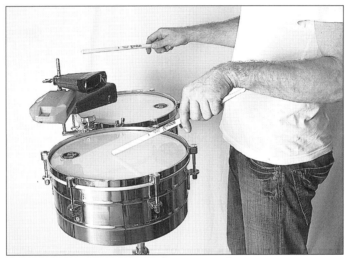

The "closed tone" (CT) segundo, using stick

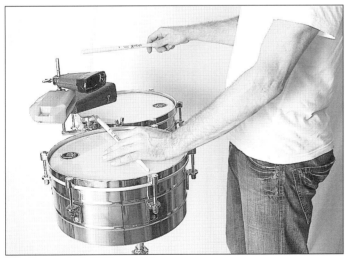

The "cross rim" (CR) segundo

The "open tone" (OT) primero

Instrumentation

Basic Rhythm Patterns for the Timbales
The Timbales in Cha-Cha-Chá

A 11, 12: Timbales Cha-Cha-Chá 1, 2
V 12, 13: Timbales Cha-Cha-Chá 1, 2

In cha-cha-chá, the right hand plays steady crotchets on the cha-cha-chá bell, which serves as the typical foundation for this rhythm. The left hand plays accents using a stick on the segundo. These accents are on 2 and 4, or 2 & and 4, respectively. Both patterns form the accompaniment on the segundo. The choice depends on the musical context and, specifically, the bass-line pattern. The accents on 2 and 2 & are muted with the stick or the hand while the accent on 4 is played open. An alternative to the muted beat on 2 or 2 & is the *cross rim*. Especially on the drum kit, this is a softer variation of the straightforward snare beat.

Another typical form of cha-cha-chá accompaniment on the timbales is the use of the rim (paila), which is an alternative to the previous segundo patterns. While the right hand plays steady crotchets on the bell, the left hand plays the written paila line on the drum shell.

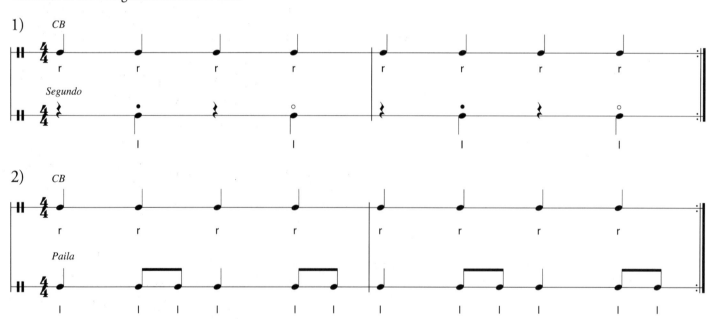

The Timbales in Mambo

A 13, 14, 15: Timbales Mambo 1, 2, 3
V 14, 15, 16: Timbales Mambo 1, 2, 3

The timbales in mambo play a slightly different role than they do in the cha-cha-chá. The signature pattern is the two-bar bell line, or *cascara* (which means "shell"), which is played with the right hand on the mambo bell. This line is written below against the 3:2 clave. (Depending on the musical context, the 2:3 version is also possible.) The left hand simultaneously plays accents on 2 and 4, or 2 & and 4, quite similar to the cha-cha-chá. These accents are divided into open and muted tones as well.

Normally, the 2 & is not additionally hit. This rhythm also has a softer variation that is used in the verse or the piano solo and played on the drum shell (also referred to as paila).

Therefore, the right hand plays the cascara on the drum shell and the left hand adds to the flow of quavers by playing the complementary rhythm. Another possibility is playing the clave pattern on a wood or jam block with the left hand while simultaneously playing the cascara on the bell or the drum shell with the right hand.

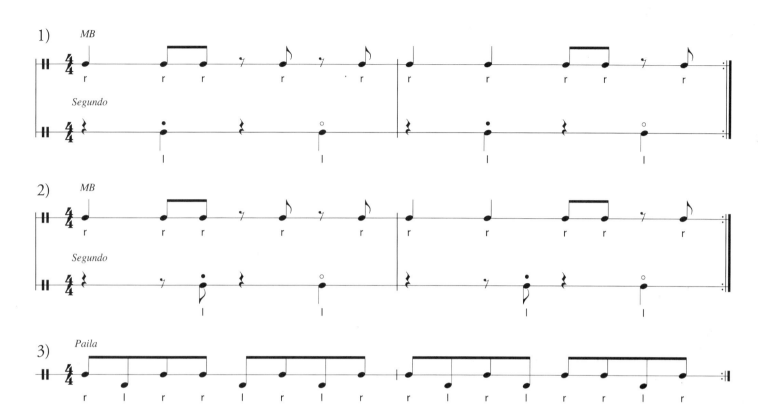

The Timbales in 6/8 or 12/8

A 16: Timbales 6/8
V 17: Timbales 6/8

The timbales in 6/8 spreads over two bars and may also be
looked at as a 12/8 line. While the right hand plays the bell
line, the left hand divides the entire figure into two equal
parts by marking the two 6/8 bars. The first "1" sounds open;
the "1" in the second bar is muted or "cross rimmed."

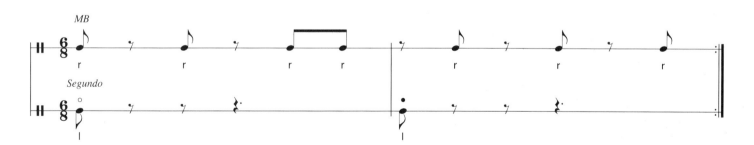

CHECKPOINT

What you've learned so far...

You have learned the basic timbale patterns for the cha-cha-chá, mambo and 6/8 time. Practise with
the play-along exercises or your own CDs. Also listen to Gloria Estefan's *Alma Caribena* or Carlos
Santana's *The Best of Santana*. See **Suggested Listening** for more great music.

The Güiro

The *güiro* (gourd scraper) is a long, hollow rhythm instrument that measures from 15 to 20 inches and is made of dried wood or dried pumpkin. The güiro is played using a 5- to 7-inch-long wooden stick, which is drawn (or scraped) over the rippled surface in both an upward and downward motion.

The Güiro

The metal version is not called a güiro but rather a *güira* (which is known today as a "torpedo").

The Güira

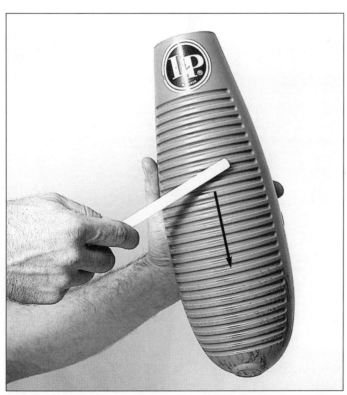

Quick downward movement

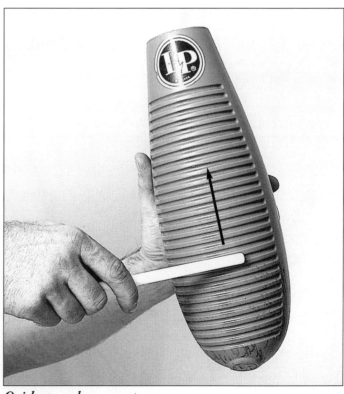

Quick upward movement

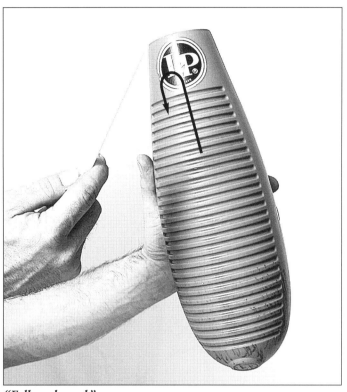

"Follow-through" movement

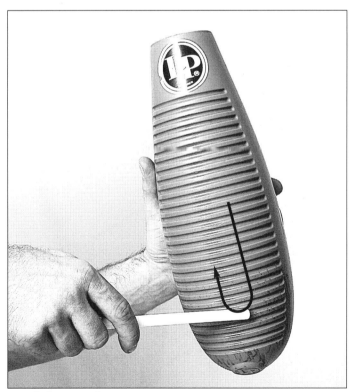

Quick downward movement

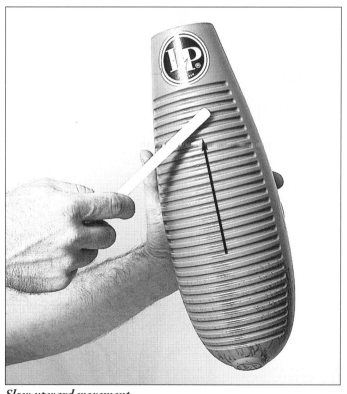

Slow upward movement

❗This instrument was used in Cuban dance orchestras back in the 1850s. The novelty that the güiro possessed was that it sounded exactly like the scraping of shuffling feet on a sanded floor.

Rhythm Patterns for the Güiro

The Güiro in 4/4

A 17: Güiro Cha-Cha-Chá 2
V 18, 19: Güiro Cha-Cha-Chá 1, 2

This basic güiro rhythm is also used in other Latin American music styles and in modern pop music. It can be played in two different ways:

1. Begin with a slow, downward movement lasting one crotchet, followed by two short upward and downward movements that equal two quavers. The direction of movement is determined by the dexterity of the player.

2. The second is a more advanced playing technique that also uses the previous pattern. The slow upward movement is anticipated by a short, crisp downward movement. These are followed by a short downward and upward movement.

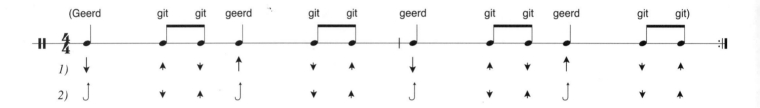

The Güiro in 6/8

A 18: Güiro 6/8
V 20: Güiro 6/8

The 6/8 pattern is quite elementary and leaves lots of room for your own creativity. Six short quaver strokes are played in a continuous upward and downward movement. At a faster tempo this rhythm can be performed by simply hitting the güiro in short quaver values.

The Maracas

The *maracas* belong to the shaker family of percussion instruments. A maraca consists of a hollow body filled with small stones, grains or seeds, and is held by a handle. The body, traditionally made from dried pumpkin, is nowadays made of wood, leather or plastic. The maracas are used in pairs and are played using a variety of techniques. You may shake them, play them with your fingertips or hit your legs with them. A soft, downward movement makes for a soft sound while a strong, downward movement causes the filling to first hit the upper part and the lower part of the body. Depending on the speed of the movement, these two sounds more or less come together to form one accentuated, simultaneous sound.

> **!** Hold the maracas as you would hold drumsticks, with your thumb resting on the "bladder" (see photo).

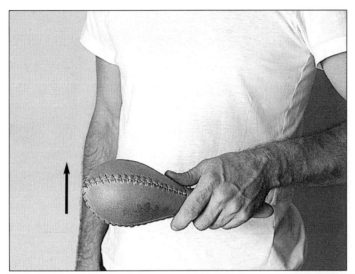
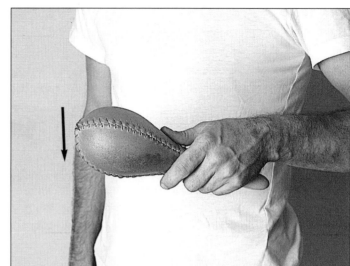

Movement for soft accent

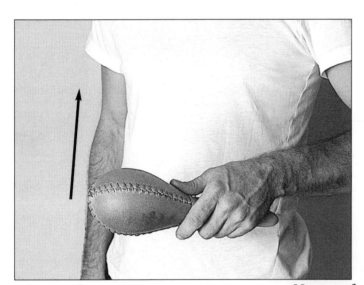
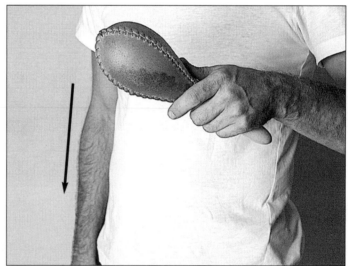

Movement for strong accent

Basic Rhythm Patterns for the Maracas
The Maracas in Cha-Cha-Chá

A 19: Maracas Cha-Cha-Chá (70 bpm)
V 21: Maracas Cha-Cha-Chá (70 bpm)

The marching character of this rhythm is emphasized by the right and left hand alternating in a quaver pattern. Normally, the strong hand accents the crotchets. Accents are added to the respective quavers on 1 &, 2, 3 & and 4 to make the rhythm sound lively.

The movement of the maracas is always vertical. The accents are made by strong upward and downward movements that cause the filling to make contact with both parts of the insides almost at the same time (as previously explained).

The Maracas in Mambo

A 20: Maracas Mambo (100 bpm)
V 22: Maracas Mambo (100 bpm)

Moving the accents to the 4 &, 1, 2 & and 3 beats
emphasizes the driving character of the mambo. The maracas
in this example are played with a slightly inclined movement,
alternating upward and downward. This creates a slightly
"off-centered" feeling that is reminiscent of rhythms like the
cha-cha-chá. This accentuation works well in a variety of
musical styles.

Basic Maracas in 6/8

A 21: Maracas 6/8
V 23: Maracas 6/8

In this example the maracas are also played with alternating
left and right hands. To emphasize the rhythmic pulse, the
first quaver of each group of three is usually accented.

> The maracas where used by both the Africans
> and the Tainos (the indigenous people of the
> Caribbean islands). Originally, one maraca was
> larger (macho) than the other (hembra).

Instrumentation

The Campana

The *campana*, or cowbell, is a trapezoid-like bell made of steel or other metals that measures 4 to 8 inches in length. This instrument is held in your weak hand and hit with a wooden stick. The campana is standard to a variety of Cuban rhythms and is often played by the bongosero. The sound definitely has a very cutting edge to it. In the cha-cha-chá and mambo rhythms it is mainly played on 1 and 3 at the mouth (M) of the bell, whereas the softer, harmonically richer sounds are made by hitting the bell further downward, near the foot (F) or heel. However, the campana will also mark steady crotchets for the dancers during the montuno (or improvisational) section of the piece.

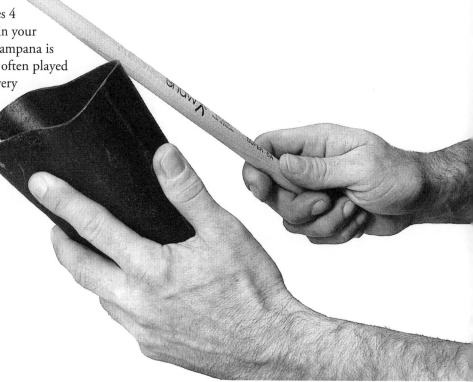

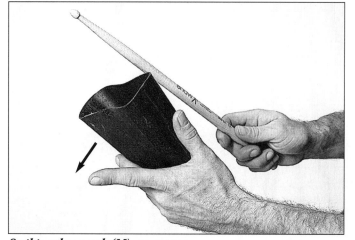

Striking the mouth (M), open tone

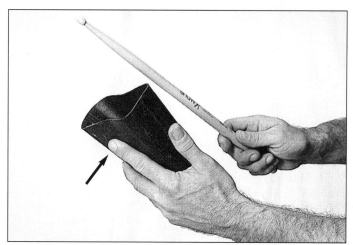

Striking the mouth (M), muted

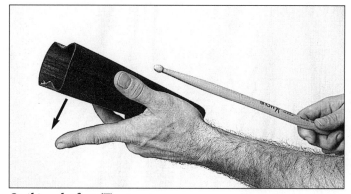

Striking the foot (F), open tone

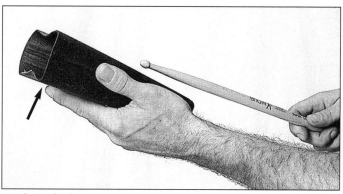

Striking the foot (F) muted

Rhythm Patterns for the Campana

Below are two standard lines for the campana which may be used in many different musical styles (rock, pop, soul or funk). The two campana lines will work well for both cha-cha-chá and mambo. The minim values on beats 1 and 3 are played strongly at the mouth (M) of the bell and the others should be played at the foot (F). Similar to the cascara line for the timbales in a previous section, this line must respect the clave rhythm. The figures below are written in the 3:2 clave pattern.

Campana Line 1

A 22: Campana 1 (70 bpm)
V 24: Campana 1 (70 bpm)

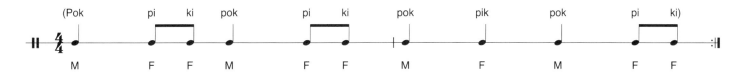

Campana Line 2

A 23: Campana 2 (100 bpm)
V 25: Campana 2 (100 bpm)

Campana in 6/8

A 24: Campana 6/8
V 26: Campana 6/8

The following line is the standard for 6/8 or 12/8 rhythms and is identical to the timbale line.

Instrumentation

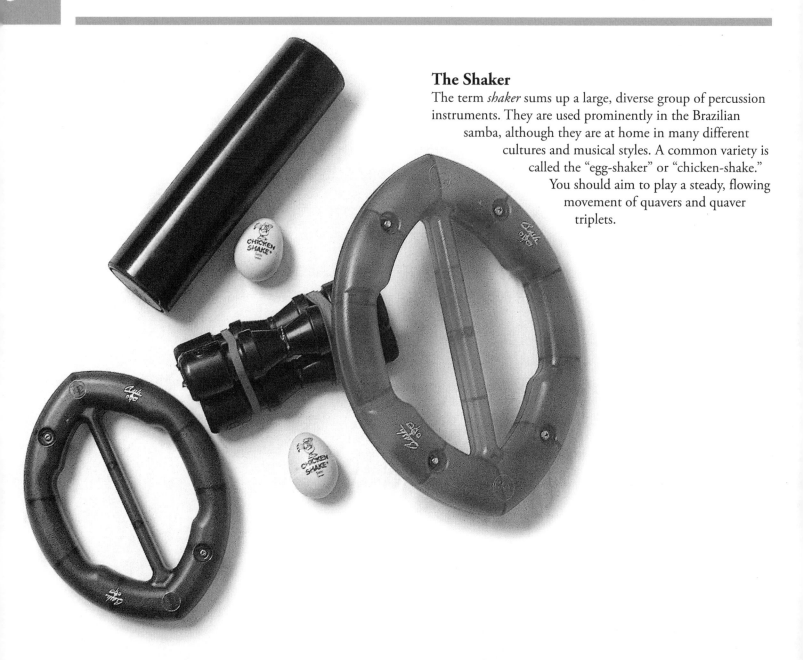

The Shaker

The term *shaker* sums up a large, diverse group of percussion instruments. They are used prominently in the Brazilian samba, although they are at home in many different cultures and musical styles. A common variety is called the "egg-shaker" or "chicken-shake." You should aim to play a steady, flowing movement of quavers and quaver triplets.

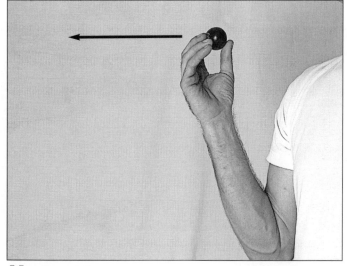

Movement 1

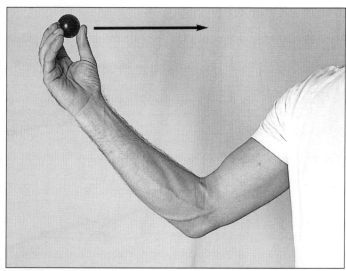

Movement 2

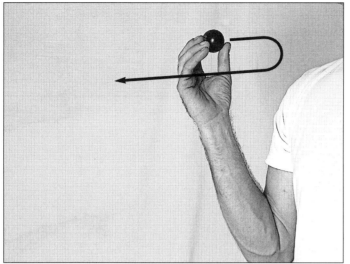

Movement 3

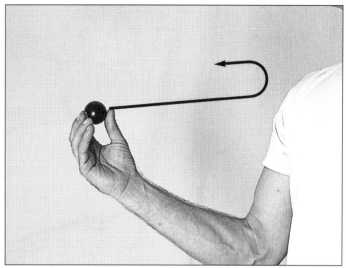

Movement 4

Rhythm Patterns for the Shaker
Basic Rhythm Pattern for the Shaker in 4/4

A 25: Shaker Pattern 1
V 27: Shaker Pattern 1

The following two rhythms should be performed with an even, horizontal movement away from and toward your body at the height of your chest.

> ❗ Shakers are used to keep time while the claves tell you where in the time you actually are.

A 26: Shaker Pattern 2
V 28: Shaker Pattern 2

Instrumentation

Rhythm No. 1 for Shaker in 6/8 or Shuffle

A 27: Shaker 6/8
V 29: Shaker 6/8

The shaker moves forward and backward across the same horizontal plane. In this example the accents create a triplet feel that coincides with these alternating movements.

Rhythm No. 2 for Shaker in Shuffle, Swing or 6/8

A 28: Shaker Shuffle
V 30: Shaker Shuffle

You may use gravity to your advantage by changing the line of movement from the horizontal to the vertical for this rhythm. That makes it easier to play this triplet-based, shuffle-type pattern.

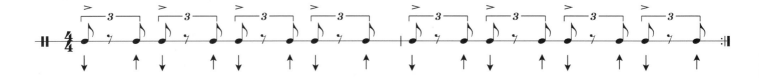

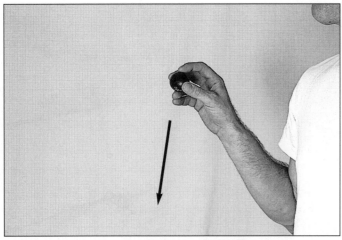

Downward movement for rhythm No. 2 Shuffle

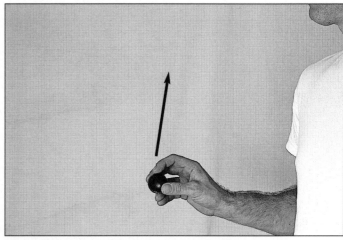

Upward movement for rhythm No. 2 Shuffle

The Tambourine

The *tambourine* consists of a round wooden frame with pairs of small metal jingles called "zils." The Brazilian version also features a skin covering one side and is called *pandeiro*. The history of the instrument has been documented back to Arabian and Muslim cultures of the 12th century.

The tambourine is played by evenly swinging the instrument back and forth. This movement creates a soft, rattling sound that can be accented by hitting the frame or skin with the lower palm of your hand. Some players also use their fingertips for additional accents, changing the movement toward the chest or upper arm.

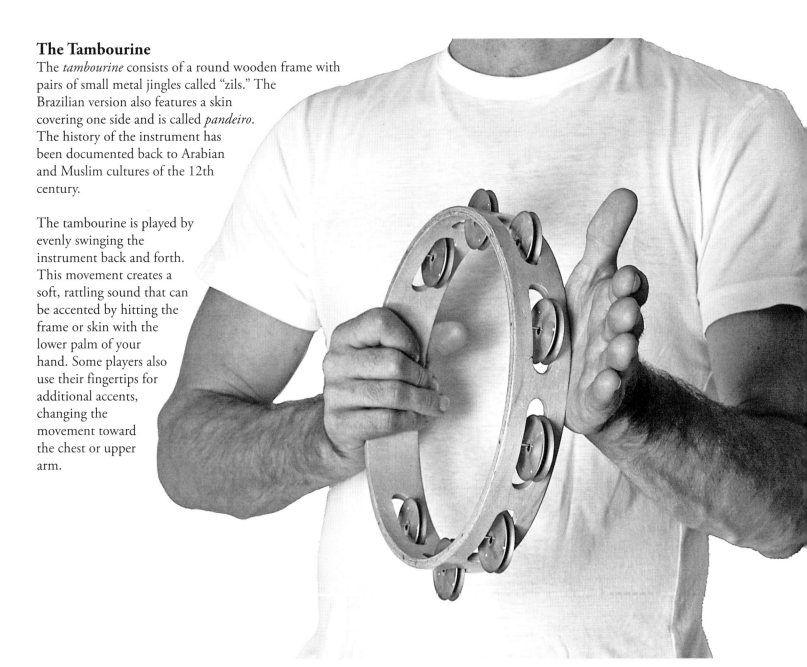

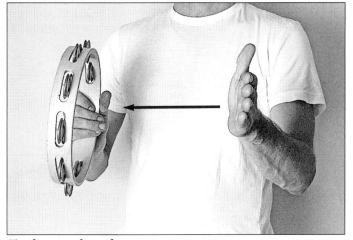

Tambourine: line of movement

! Mozart used the tambourine in his German dances, composed in 1787.

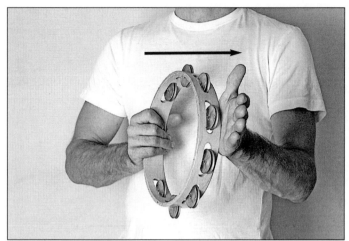

Tambourine movement: accent with low palm (LP)

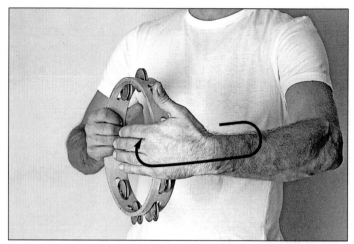

Tambourine movement: accent with fingertips (FT)

Rhythm Patterns for the Tambourine

Basic Rhythm Pattern for the Tambourine in 4/4

To play figures 1 and 2, simply move the tambourine evenly
back and forth in a horizontal line at the height of your chest.
Remember to use your free hand to tap the frame and create
different accents.

A 29: Tambourine Pattern 1
V 31: Tambourine Pattern 1

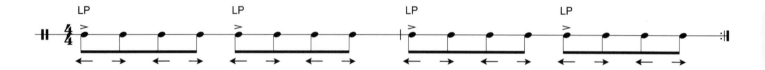

A 30: Tambourine Pattern 2
V 32: Tambourine Pattern 2

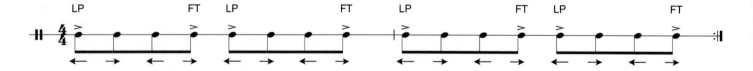

Rhythm No. 1 in 6/8 or Shuffle

A 31: Tambourine 6/8
V 33: Tambourine 6/8

You can use the fingertip accent for emphasizing the downbeats of this rhythm. The playing movement also takes place across a horizontal line. Notice that, as with the shaker, the accents alternate with the forward and backward movements.

! Try using the fingertip accent on both sides of the frame. This will help create syncopated patterns.

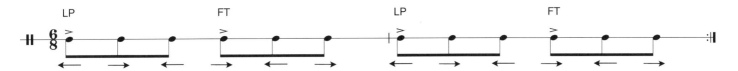

Rhythm No.2 in Shuffle, Swing or 6/8

A 32: Tambourine Shuffle
V 34: Tambourine Shuffle

Try this rhythm pattern with the "backswing" (see photo below). This line of movement becomes slightly vertical and adds a crisper sound to the typical shuffle groove.

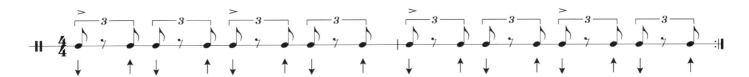

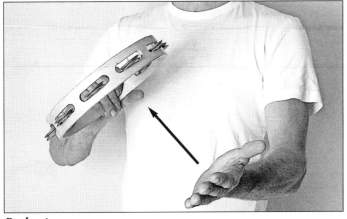

Backswing

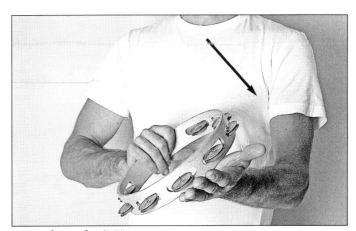

Accent low palm (LP)

CHECKPOINT

What you've learned so far...

You've become familiar with the most important hand percussion instruments in Cuban music. In addition, you've learned rhythm patterns that you can now use to enhance any style of music from Latin to pop.

Interplay of Voices

The Cha-Cha-Chá

The cha-cha-chá came to prominence in the 1950s, and is known all over the world. Its popularity has resulted in crossover blending with jazz and pop music. Artists responsible for this phenomenon are guitar great Carlos Santana and the legendary timbalero/band leader Tito Puente.

Since 1961, the cha-cha-chá has been accepted as a Latin-American ballroom dance which has also added to its favourable acceptance. The music is based on a 4/4 rhythm that is slow in tempo but strongly played.

The Separate Voices of the Cha-Cha-Chá in the Verse (Pregón)

A 33: Cha-Cha-Chá verse (70 bpm)

The verse is normally the softer part of a tune and therefore should be dynamically lighter. For all percussion instruments this means to "bring the volume down!"

The timbales can be played on the shell (paila) instead of the segundo. In addition, the congas can simply play the tumbao only while the bongosero focuses his rhythm pattern to just the bongos.

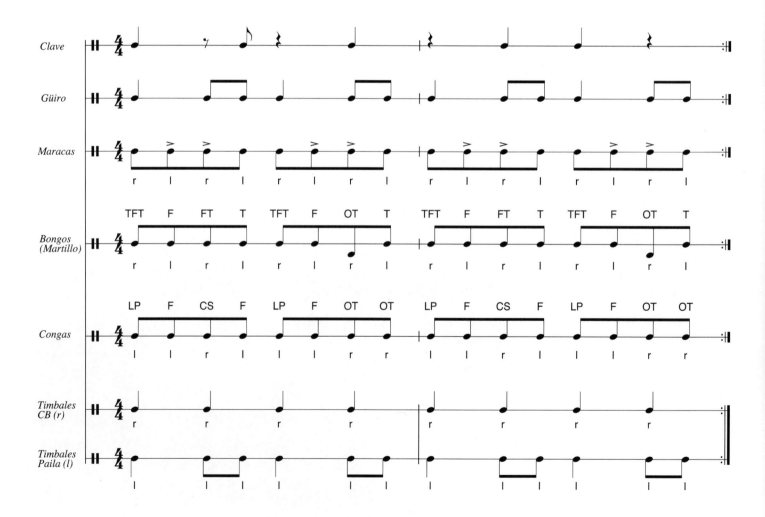

Separate Voices of the Cha-Cha-Chá in the Chorus (Córo)

A 34: Cha-Cha-Chá chorus (70 bpm)

The chorus is the louder part of the tune, so it doesn't come as a surprise that the musicians generally bring up the volume in this section. The timbalero may return to the segundo, the congero adds the salidor and the bongosero switches to the campana.

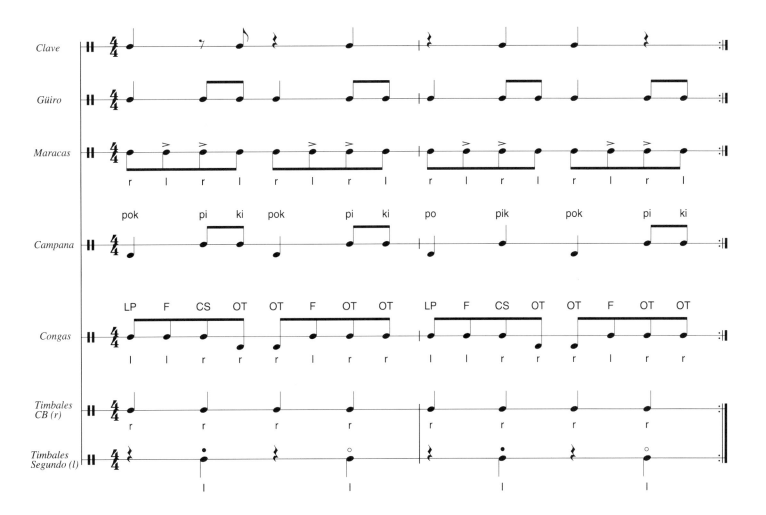

Interplay of Voices

The Mambo

Mambo is a style of music and dance that was developed after 1930 in Cuba. The immigration of many Latin Americans to the United States—especially to New York City during and after the Second World War—brought with it the assimilation of Cuban rhythms to jazz (Dizzy Gillespie) and pop (Elvis Presley). The inverse was also true as jazz began to influence mambo in a way that can be heard even in today's salsa styles.

Separate Voices of the Mambo in the Verse (Pregón)

A 35: Mambo verse (100 bpm)

Once again, the verse is meant to be played a little softer in order to make the lyrics of the song easily understood. The congas should take down the volume, or change to the one-bar tumbao figure while the timbales play in the paila-style, and the bongos reflect the relaxed martillo rhythm.

Separate Voices of the Mambo in the Chorus (Córo)

A 36: Mambo chorus (100 bpm)

The timbalero changes to the bell in conjunction with the segundo while the bongosero switches from the bongos to the campana. The congero brings in the tumbadora into his new pattern that is now two bars long.

A Popular Pattern for the 6/8 Rhythm

Although the 6/8 rhythm already belongs to the category of compound meters, it is possible to add a popular, relatively advanced pattern, since this rhythm is very common in Latin American music. Don't hesitate to vary your playing in favour of a more individualistic sound and touch. However, always keep in mind that these flights of fancy should add to the flavour of the music in an appropriate manner.

Interplay of Voices

Separate Voices of the 6/8 Rhythm Pattern Combined

A 37: 6/8 Pattern

There is only one example of accompaniment for 6/8 here. It is strongly suggested that you vary the dynamics between the verse, chorus and solo sections. In addition, there are some instrumental variations that are not only possible but common:

1. Alternating between maracas and güiro.
2. Replacing the bongos with a second handbell.
3. The timbalero can change from the segundo to the paila.

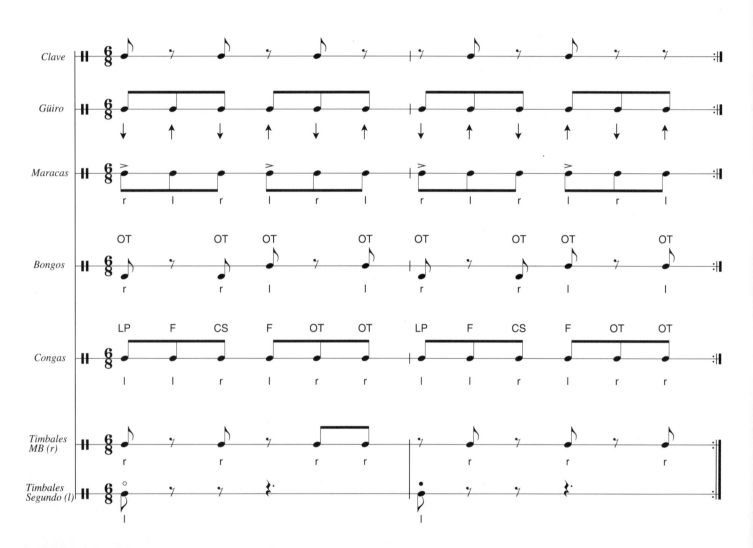

CHECKPOINT

What you have learned so far...

You now know the most significant instruments used in Latin American music. In addition, you understand that the cha-cha-chá and mambo consist of different sections (pregón and córo), which you can now accompany appropriately. If you listen to a lot of different salsa and pop music, you'll recognize the rhythmic figures that you've learned in this book.

General Exercises

Before entering this rhythmic world of music, it is suggested—as with every other instrument—to begin with different warm-up exercises. Generally speaking, you should go through the exercises slowly at first. Tempo will come naturally as you become more comfortable and your playing improves.

Use other people's ideas as well as your own because, apart from lots of rules, it's the music that counts in the end, and creative, original playing is the element that makes this music come alive. Play along with all your favourite CDs (remember to choose slower tempos in the beginning). You'll soon notice that even a simple exercise can develop into an original rhythm.

About the Clave

As with the campana, you can immediately start playing the rhythms. The most important consideration is exact timing, as the playing technique shouldn't take long to get used to. It is suggested that you try tapping out the crotchets with a military march-style movement of your feet (1–2–3–4; left and right), while at the same time clapping the quaver values (1–&–2–&–3–&–4–&) with your hands. Also, try saying the numbers out loud. Of course, the &s are the most difficult, and are appropriately called the "off" beats.

About the Congas

The sound of the conga rhythms depends mostly on the sound produced by the technical quality of the single strokes. Try practising quavers at first and mix them with other note values later on. You should aim to create a good tone from the congas while maintaining even strokes as you play. Then you can begin adding combinations of slaps and open tones using different note values.

After this becomes somewhat comfortable, you can now move on to certain variations; for example, play the rhythm for three bars in a row and vary the next bar with different stroke and note-value combinations. The see-saw motion of the floating-hand technique may be combined with open tones and slaps in the right hand. These can also be applied to exercises that are three or four beats long, such as LP–F–CS, LP–F–OT, LP–F–OT–OT, and so on.

Tips and Tricks

About the Bongos

The martillo is by far the most popular rhythm for the bongos and offers almost endless possibilities. Single strokes can be practised effectively in two-beat sections by playing the first four strokes or the second four strokes separately. Later on they are combined to play the full rhythm.

The lying thumb on 4 & and 2, and following strokes FT, are very important for the sound of the rhythm. These FTs should sound very high and cutting since the thumb strokes prepare the important beats 1 and 3. You should also end your combination of strokes on 4 & for now. This will prepare you to start the rhythm pattern on the next downbeat of 1. Later on, you'll be able to easily combine rhythms and variations within one bar.

About the Timbales

When playing the timbales, you might be using sticks for the first time. Use a firm grip with your thumb and index finger while making a kind of fist with your other finger. For the cha-cha-chá, you play even crotchets with the right hand. The left hand accents the 2 (or 2 &) with a muted stroke, and the 4 with an open-sounding stroke. This segundo variation should be practised and mastered separately before trying out the combination.

You may also try other rhythmic variations, with the steady crotchets holding the rhythm together. The mambo line requires you to play the cascara on the bell or the paila. Later on, you may place accents on the 2, 2 & and 4 with your left hand. To understand this complicated line better, try to play it with your right hand while the left hand fills in the gaps to create a steady quaver pattern.

About the Güiro

The basic form of güiro playing consists of only three fundamental movements:

1. The quick stroke (an up/down movement).
2. The slow stroke (also an up/down movement).
3. A quick downstroke followed by a slow upward movement.

The playing hand should move from the wrist with some strength. It's important to practise the strokes separately at first. Once you're comfortable with the three movements you can then put them together for the complete rhythm.

About the Maracas

Practise the quick but loose movement of each maraca from the wrist with a downward motion. The tempo should be slow at first, with the filling touching only the lower inside of the shell. Next, you can make the downward movement stronger, resulting in the filling touching both insides of the shell. This produces a thick, accented tone.

Try these two basic exercises:
1. Four loud and four soft strokes, alternately.
2. Two loud and two soft strokes, alternately.

Then, mix them up for some variation.

About the Campana

Begin by immediately playing the rhythms. Strokes on mouth and foot should be executed smoothly. The hand that holds the bell moves up and down slightly from the wrist towards the stroke.

About the Shakers

The ultimate goal when playing the shaker is to achieve an even forward-and-backward movement. Try this without any accents at first. Then you can begin adding single accents to the movement (notice that the backward accents are more difficult to play).

Practise following up the backward accent with a forward accent while trying to maintain your even flow of playing. At first, practise playing accents by hitting your free hand with the shaker. When playing the shuffle technique (vertical movement), you can vary the crispness of attack by tilting the line of movement.

About the Tambourine

The things said about the shaker apply equally to the tambourine, with the exception of movement being sideways, rather than forward and backward. For accents, you may use either the palm of your hand, your chest or the lower arm of your free hand.

Again, the most important thing is to keep a steady rhythm. For this reason, you shouldn't make the accents too heavy, as this might compromise the rhythmic flow. Also, the same concept applies for the vertical movement of the shaker.

Tips and Tricks

About Playing Music

The first step toward playing music is much easier than you might think. Begin by listening to a well-known piece of music and play the rhythms and exercises along with what you hear. At first, you should go for slower tempos and focus on loosening up your muscles every once in a while. Let the music carry you along while trying out some variations. Don't worry about getting lost—just stop, listen, and find your way back into the groove.

You will soon recognize the advantages of this kind of practising. Playing along with recordings of great musicians—who won't give you a hard time if you happen to make a mistake here or there—is a great place to start. But don't wait too long before you start playing with real musicians, because there's nothing more satisfying than communicating with other people through music. For starters, the ideal setting for this could be an informal gathering of familiar people, also known as a "living room jam."

Practice Tips

How much should I practise? This is the single most important question in terms of musical development. There's no one answer to this question but regular, daily practice goes a very long way. Aim for 15 minutes a day rather than a few hours on Sundays only. The tempo of the music you play along with should always match your technical abilities.

If you have problems, practise alone, using a metronome. Make sure that you are comfortable with your practising situation and tempo at all times. Be sure to take regular breaks and keep a relaxed posture.

Choosing an Instrument

As with every other instrument, you should ask yourself some fundamental questions before actually going into the shop and buying, such as: How much money do I want to spend? What surrounding am I going to use my instrument in? Am I really sure about my chosen instrument?

Every major brand offers a professional and a beginner level instrument. The price of a reasonable set of congas comes down to about £300. Of course, the same can be had for as little as £200. You should pay attention to the diameter of the drums. For adults, 11" and 11 3/4" are recommended; for kids, 10 1/4" and 11" might be quite sufficient. In each case, the hands should have enough space to perform all the playing techniques on the drums.

Congas and bongos are available in wood and fibreglass. These materials have different effects on the instrument's sound quality. Wooden instruments normally have a warmer, more mellow sound while fibreglass gives a cutting edge to the sound, as well as being well suited to the "wear and tear" of touring on the road. Personal taste should be the utmost consideration.

You might want to use stands, depending on whether you prefer standing up or sitting down while playing. Aside from that, a stand allows the conga to resonate more deeply, since it now "hovers" above the ground.

Basically, the same applies to the bongos. Prices range from £20 to £200, whereas everything under £30 can't really be taken seriously. The timbales range between £100 and £500. You should look for sturdy metal shells and extra heads (skins).

Creativity

Creative and original playing is the key to musical success. Not only is it important to master the rhythms for each instrument, but it is equally important to add an original, personal touch to everything you play. The most important asset in this direction is experimenting and trying out as much as you can. In this manner, lots of ideas may not be "right" or "wrong"—it's your musical taste that determines whether they do or do not fit the music.

Try leaving the rhythm and coming back again—another principle of popular improvisational music. If you play a fill that doesn't quite "make it," try again and again until you're happy with it and make it a part of your repertoire. This may be applied to all other instruments, as well as trying out things you hear from maybe the guitar or the voice. Pay attention not to "overplay" or play too much (less is often more), and give your fellow musicians the space they need to develop their own musical ideas.

Appendix

Suggested Listening

Cha-Cha-Chá

Tito Puente – *Son con Son (Mambo King)*
Tito Puente – *Jo Je Ji (On Broadway)*
Santana – *Oye como va (Best of)*
Poncho Sanchez – *Sonando (Bailar Live)*
Poncho Sanchez – *Mas! (Bien Sabroso)*
Carlos "Patato" Valdes – *Comelon (Masterpiece)*
Mario Bauzá – *Asi no, Papa (My Time Is Now)*
The Color of Latin Jazz – *Linda Chicana (From Samba to Bomba)*
Santana – *Smooth (Supernatural)*
Dave Samuels – *Soul Sauce (Tjaderized)*

6/8 or 12/8

Giovanni Hidalgo – *Villa Hidalgo (Villa Hidalgo)*
Cal Tjader – *Afro Blue (Cal Tjader Sextet)*
Poncho Sanchez – *Alafia (Bailar Live)*
Cassandra Wilson – *Estrellas (Blue Light 'Til Dawn)*
Sergio Mendes – *Pipoca (Brasileiro)*
Mario Bauzá – *Chano (944 Columbus)*
Dave Samuels – *Triste (Tjaderized)*
Andy Narell – *Jenny's Room (The Long Time Band)*
Santana – *Red Prophet (Milagro)*

Mambo

Mario Bauzá – *Jack the Knife (My Time Is Now)*
Gloria Estefan – *Si Senor! (Mi Tierra)*
Dizzy Gillespie – *Manteca (The Giant)*
Poncho Sanchez – *Baila (Keeper of the Flame)*
Charlie Palmieri – *Mambo Show (Latin Bugalu)*
Dave Samuel – *Bachi (Tjaderized)*
Eddie Palmieri – *Solito (Solito)*
Mario Bauzá – *Azulito (Tanga)*
Mongo Santamaria – *Breaking it in (Costa del Oro)*
Carlos "Patato" Valdes – *Marcoris (Unico y Diferente)*
Tito Puente – *Woody 'N You (Tito's Idea)*

Soul/Pop/Funk/Rock

Babyface – Various titles *(Unplugged)*
Earth, Wind & Fire – Various titles *(Unplugged & Live)*
Sade – Various titles *(Diamond Life)*
Miles Davis – Various titles *(Fast Track)*
George Benson – Various titles *(Weekend in L.A.)*
Michael Franks – Various titles *(Blue Pacific)*
Jackie Terrasson & Cassandra Wilson – Various titles *(Rendezvous)*
Sting – Various titles *(Nothing Like The Sun)*
John Patitucci – Various titles *(Another World)*
Toto – Various titles *(Absolutely Live)*

Terminology

Groove:	steady rhythmic pulse or beat
Pattern:	a certain rhythmic line
Son:	traditional Cuban music (see "Pregón")
Montuno:	the córo part of Cuban music
Abakuá:	a traditional Cuban form of rhythm
Córo:	the chorus of a song
Drumset:	"the drums" as known in pop music today
Segundo:	the lower timbale
Primero:	the higher timbale
Macho:	the smaller bongó
Hembra:	the lower bongó
BPM:	beats per minute
Real Time:	the original tempo
Double-Time:	double the original tempo
Half-Time:	half the original tempo

About the Author

Hilko Schomerus began playing in 1982 and enlisted in Freddie Santiago's Percussion Academia for one year in 1987. In 1989 he founded the percussion school Tres Golpes in Hanover, Germany. Today, he works as a studio musician and performing artist, as well as a drum teacher and percussion instructor. He has also been an artist-in-residence in Venezuela, Ghana, Mexico and Indonesia, among others.

Further activities:

Member of teaching staff at AfS, VdS, Remscheid Academy, Hanover Music High School, Cologne Music High School, Detmold College of Music, Hamburg College of Music, PCC Cologne, Percussion Creativ.

He has worked with:

Randy Crawford, Quincy Jones, Phil Collins, Fury in the Slaughterhouse, Hiram Bullock, Bootsie Collins, Fred Wesley, Lamont Dozier, Dave Liebman, Cunnie Williams, Backstreet, Gamut of Crimc, Camerata Freden, Cultured Pearls, Mousse T., Gregor Prächt, Echt, Inga Rumpf, JUJU Orchestra, among others.

For more information about the world of percussion and also about the author, please visit:
http://www.10dance.de

Acknowledgements

First of all, I'd like to thank all of my students. In addition, thanks to LP Latin Percussion, Schlagwerk Percussion, and Roland Electronic Percussion for their support. Lastly, of course, my treasured colleagues and friends, such as: Ralf Larmann, Christof Litmann (Keyboards and Bass), Marc Collazzo, Freddie Santiago, Prof. Andreas Böttger, and Prof. Jürgen Terhag.

Audio and Video Track Listing

The included CD can be played on a CD Player or a computer. The audio CD features all of the audio demos: tracks 1–37. From track 38 on, you'll find some arrangements (full version and play-along), that will be fun to jam along with. Listen to the full version first before you jam with the play-along. The very first clave that you learned will help to guide you through.

When you open the CD on the computer, you'll find two additional data files. The first file contains all the tracks from the audio CD at faster tempos in the MP3 format. The second file contains videos for you to watch and learn. Here, all the movements are explicitly demonstrated. Watch the video that goes with every rhythm as this is the quickest and most effective way to learn.

Audio demos on CD

1   3:2 Son Clave (70 bpm)
2   § Clave (70 bpm)
3   Congas Cuban Tumbao (70 bpm)
4   Congas § Tumbao (70 bpm)
5   Congas Swing Tumbao (70 bpm)
6   Congas Cha-Cha-Chá (70 bpm)
7   Congas Mambo (100 bpm)
8   Bongos Martillo Cha-Cha-Chá (70 bpm)
9   Bongos Martillo Mambo (100 bpm)
10 Bongos § (70 bpm)
11 Timbales 1 Cha-Cha-Chá (70 bpm)
12 Timbales 2 Cha-Cha-Chá (70 bpm)
13 Timbales 1 Mambo (100 bpm)
14 Timbales 2 Mambo (100 bpm)
15 Timbales 3 (Paila) Mambo (100 bpm)
16 Timbales § (70 bpm)
17 Güiro Cha-Cha-Chá 2 (70 bpm)
18 Güiro § (70 bpm)
19 Maracas Cha-Cha-Chá (70 bpm)
20 Maracas Mambo (100 bpm)
21 Maracas § (70 bpm)
22 Campana 1 (70 bpm)
23 Campana 2 (100 bpm)
24 Campana § (70 bpm)
25 Shaker Pattern 1 (70 bpm)
26 Shaker Pattern 2 (70 bpm)
27 Shaker § (70 bpm)
28 Shaker Shuffle (70 bpm)
29 Tambourine Pattern 1 (70 bpm)
30 Tambourine Pattern 2 (70 bpm)
31 Tambourine § (70 bpm)
32 Tambourine Shuffle (70 bpm)
33 Cha-Cha-Chá Verse (70 bpm)
34 Cha-Cha-Chá Chorus (70 bpm)
35 Mambo Verse (100 bpm)
36 Mambo Chorus (100 bpm)
37 § Pattern (70 bpm)
38 Cha-Cha-Chá Arrangement (70 bpm)
39 Cha-Cha-Chá Arrangement Playback
40 Mambo Arrangement (100 bpm)
41 Mambo Arrangement Playback
42 § Arrangement (70 bpm)
43 § Arrangement Playback

Audio demos in MP3 format

1   3:2 Son Clave (100 bpm, 140 bpm)
2   § Clave (100 bpm)
3   Congas Cuban Tumbao (100 bpm, 140 bpm)
4   Congas § Tumbao (100 bpm)
5   Congas Swing Tumbao (100 bpm)
6   Congas Cha-Cha-Chá (100 bpm)
7   Congas Mambo (140 bpm)
8   Bongos Martillo Cha-Cha-Chá (100 bpm)
9   Bongos Martillo Mambo (140 bpm)
10 Bongos § (100 bpm)
11 Timbales 1 Cha-Cha-Chá (100 bpm)
12 Timbales 2 Cha-Cha-Chá (100 bpm)
13 Timbales 1 Mambo (140 bpm)
14 Timbales 2 Mambo (140 bpm)
15 Timbales 3 (Paila) Mambo (140 bpm)
16 Timbales § (100 bpm)
17 Güiro Cha-Cha-Chá 2 (100 bpm, 140 bpm)
18 Güiro § (100 bpm)
19 Maracas Cha-Cha-Chá (100 bpm)
20 Maracas Mambo (140 bpm)
21 Maracas § (100 bpm)
22 Campana 1 (100 bpm, 140 bpm)
23 Campana 2 (140 bpm)
24 Campana 6/8 (100 bpm)
25 Shaker Pattern 1 (100 bpm)
26 Shaker Pattern 2 (100 bpm)
27 Shaker § (100 bpm)
28 Shaker Shuffle (100 bpm)
29 Tambourine Pattern 1 (100 bpm)
30 Tambourine Pattern 2 (100 bpm)
31 Tambourine § (100 bpm)
32 Tambourine Shuffle (100 bpm)
33 Cha-Cha-Chá Verse (100 bpm)
34 Cha-Cha-Chá Chorus (100 bpm)
35 Mambo Verse (140 bpm)
36 Mambo Chorus (140 bpm)
37 § Pattern (100 bpm)
38 Cha-Cha-Chá Arrangement (100 bpm)
39 Cha-Cha-Chá Arrangement Playback
40 Mambo Arrangement (140 bpm)
41 Mambo Arrangement Playback
42 § Arrangement (100 bpm)
43 § Arrangement Playback

Quicktime Videos

1   3:2 Son Clave
2   § Clave
3   Congas Cuban Tumbao
4   Congas Modern Tumbao
5   Congas § Tumbao
6   Congas Swing Tumbao
7   Congas Cha-Cha-Chá
8   Congas Mambo
9   Bongos Cha-Cha-Chá
10 Bongos Mambo
11 Bongos §
12 Timbales Cha-Cha-Chá 1
13 Timbales Cha-Cha-Chá 2
14 Timbales Mambo 1
15 Timbales Mambo 2
16 Timbales Mambo 3
17 Timbales §
18 Güiro Cha-Cha-Chá 1
19 Güiro Cha-Cha-Chá 2
20 Güiro §
21 Maracas Cha-Cha-Chá
22 Maracas Mambo
23 Maracas §
24 Campana 1
25 Campana 2
26 Campana §
27 Shaker Pattern 1
28 Shaker Pattern 2
29 Shaker §
30 Shaker Shuffle
31 Tambourine Pattern 1
32 Tambourine Pattern 2
33 Tambourine §
34 Tambourine Shuffle

To remove your CD from the plastic sleeve, lift the small lip to break the perforations. Replace the disc after use for convenient storage.